Time Management Strategies

Learn How to Stop Procrastination and Master Productivity Hacks to Gain Self-Confidence, Self-Discipline Hacks for Leadership Habit Stacking & Greater Joy in Life

By

Nick Jones

Table of Contents

Introduction

Time management is an important skill that determines whether you succeed in life or not. You have an infinite amount of time. What you do with it today will determine how much of it you can enjoy in your later years.

You have dreams and aspirations that you want to come true at some point in the foreseeable future. These dreams can only come true if you devote your time and energy towards making them a reality. Procrastination is one of the biggest threats standing in your way. A lot of people struggle with it, very few ever own up to it.

Procrastination is nothing to be ashamed of. People have been procrastinating since the beginning of time. However, those people are not in your future. They are not in your plans, and they do not feature anywhere in your goals.

You have tools in your grasp that can help you to win the war against procrastination. You have access to tools and systems that will help you be organized, focused, and allow you to change the way you go about your day. By changing your perspective, you have a better shot at realizing your dreams earlier than you had planned. This also means you have more time to enjoy your success.

In this book, you will learn some of the challenges people endure each day, and how to deal with them. You will learn simple steps that you can take, changes that you can utilize in your daily plan, and therefore realize huge returns. You will master the art of improving your productivity. This is not rocket science, but simple, reasonable, and achievable things that you can do.

At the end of this book, you will have realized where you lose time, some of the things you do which are unnecessary, and how to win back your time. You will learn how to start your day the right way. You will learn how to end a hectic day without feeling frustrated. You have the tools to help you be more productive at work, improve the quality of your life, and gain self-confidence.

You have all the tools you need to become successful in life, and all you need to do is manage your time!

Chapter 1: What is Time Management?

If you ever want to succeed in all aspects of your life, you must understand and appreciate the importance of time. In the recent past, you have heard a lot of people mock and ridicule a popular phrase about everyone having 24 hours a day. This is a statement often made by people who seem to have made it in life, encouraging others to use their hours in the day wisely.

There are different ways to look at this. For a fact, someone who has many people working for them in various aspects of their day honestly does not have the same 24 hours as someone who is doing everything on their own. If you have people working for you, you have a few hours from each of them every day, so your level of productivity is different from someone who works on their own.

However, there is still a lesson in time management here. It is very easy to have lots of people lending you their hours daily but still fail to achieve anything noteworthy. Other than the element of altruism that comes with that statement, one thing that you should take from it is the importance of time management.

Time management refers to your ability to use your time wisely and effectively so that you apportion the right time to the right activities. This is primarily about priorities and goals. Like most resources, time is limited, and you must use it wisely. You do not want to wake up one day and wonder why you are not making progress in life.

In time management, you have to prioritize tasks in order of their importance, allocate more time to jobs that demand more time, and so forth. Do not spend a lot of time on things that you can get done in a short amount of time. Time management is not just something you practice to appease your employers or your workmates, but it is something that, when you master it, will be very important, even in your personal life.

The following are some of the elements that are involved in time management, which will help you to make the most use of your day, and to become more productive if you handle them well:

Goals and Objectives

If you do not have any goals or objectives, what are you working to achieve? You would be no different than a captain of a ship wandering at sea, allowing the wind to take him wherever it pleases.

By setting goals and objectives, you are merely giving yourself targets that you have to achieve. Meeting these targets goes a long way towards making sure you succeed in life. It is the little milestones you accomplish that eventually set you apart from everyone else.

Besides, having something to work towards also helps you account for your time. You know at the end of the day whether it has been a success or not, given how much of what you set out to do you have accomplished. This also helps you determine how much more you need to do the next day in case you did not manage to complete all your tasks for the day, or if you need to put in extra hours that evening to push results.

Effective Planning

Managing your time also calls for effective planning. Planning is about preparing a blueprint for the day, and how to go about it. When you set goals and objectives, you have already determined your destination for the day. With planning, you decide how to get there.

Like most people, you might have many things that you need to get done before that day is over. However, you cannot achieve them all at once. You need to find a way of accomplishing each task one by one.

You must allocate the right amount of time to each task. Plan for the challenging tasks earlier on in your day, while you are still fresh and have the energy to tackle them accordingly. Unless you have completed a job, do not start on something else. It is always wise to finish one task before moving on to another, lest you end up with a pile of uncompleted tasks, which can lead to confusion.

Deadlines

One thing that is obvious with plans and setting goals and objectives is a deadline. You need a timeline within which you have to complete a specific task. You cannot do one thing forever unless you have mastered the art of procrastination, which is eventually detrimental to your life.

While planning is vital to meet your goals and objectives, setting deadlines is equally essential. Deadlines help you to push your limits, get that drive needed to get you across the finish line. Working hard enough to beat your deadlines is critical.

Meeting or beating deadlines usually makes you feel good about yourself, bestows some self-confidence upon you and, in some cases, even makes you feel invincible. You also get to know how well you perform under pressure, and whether you can channel this to better use.

If you consistently set deadlines for all the work you set out to accomplish each day, you will soon have a good idea of how much time to spend on each task. Over time, you can confidently give assurances on how much time you need for any assigned work, and therefore become a dependable person.

Delegating Duties and Responsibilities

However much you love to believe you can succeed on your own, that is a lie. Success is a collaborative effort. You must learn and be willing to work with those around you to succeed in life.

There are things that you will have to delegate to others

to help you achieve the higher goal. You must learn to build a successful team around you, a group of people who are capable, focused, and working towards the same goal as you.

The delegation of duties is an integral part of time management. You set aside tasks for people around you depending on their abilities and skills. You must, therefore, understand and know their strengths and weaknesses. Specialization in itself is a strength you must possess. Assigning the right duties to the right person and at the right time allows you to achieve your goals faster.

Remember that point we mentioned earlier about having the same 24 hours? It is not just about literally having 24 hours in a day. It is about managing the 24 hours that people in your circle offer you over the course of a day.

Setting Priorities

What is more important and what is it on your list of things to do that can be achieved much later? Time management is also about setting priorities. Some things have to be completed before others.

When it comes to priorities, you need to understand the

difference between urgent stuff and important stuff. Something might be compelling, but it is not essential. In this case, you can shelve it for a while, given the nature of your goals for that day.

When setting priorities, you have to look at your goals and objectives. What tasks do you feel need to be given top priority, considering what you want to achieve in the long run? By setting priorities, you also have a better shot at creating an effective plan for your day.

Spending Time Wisely

Since you already have things worked out, how you go about them will make a big difference. Your goals and objectives are clear. You have prioritized the tasks on how to accomplish them, and you already have a plan. All you need is to set things in motion and check them off your list one by one.

You need to know how much time each activity demands. Get into the habit of doing things at the right time and completing them when they are supposed to be. There is a good reason why you should be completing some tasks as and when you are supposed to.

More often than not, tasks that you complete later than they were supposed to eventually have no use. You will have ended up wasting a lot of your time in the process. Why are you spending a whole day working on something you can finish in an hour? You will not just be wasting time on that task, but you will have wasted time on other things too. Time wastage sets you back because your work will spill over into the next day, which means you start that day on the backfoot.

Respecting Personal Time

Do you give your personal time the respect it deserves? Do you even plan for personal time? The importance and need for private time is lost on a lot of people. Even if they do make time for it, they do not know what to do with it.

So, what is personal time? Personal time is the period you set aside for yourself. It is time you check your social media profiles and do other things not related to your schedules or goals for the day. This time demands as much respect as the time you devote to your work.

Taking personal time is essential as it helps you rejuvenate and feel fresh. It helps you to learn to be a friendly person. You do not exist in isolation. You cannot wish away the impact of social media and other things that your social circles involve. These are important contributions to your overall wellbeing.

You should set aside this time away from your work hours so that you do not interfere with your productivity. It is easy to delve into social media and get carried away. A few minutes of checking out an interesting photo or post could lead to spending hours of your day reading interesting long threads on Twitter or Facebook, and before you know it, the day is gone.

Effective Time Management

To succeed at effective time management, you must organize yourself. You must learn to follow instructions, at least starting with the ones you set out for yourself. There is an order of doing things that you must immerse yourself into. Start your day early. Starting early helps a great deal. Starting your day early means that you also sleep early.

Early in the morning, get a few minutes of exercise. Exercise will give your body that jolt of energy that keeps you going. Have some fruits or fresh juice in the morning, or whatever it is that keeps you fully energized. Do something constructive even in your free time. Read a book.

Have a positive mindset. Avoid all defeatist thoughts. When you set out to achieve anything, go about it knowing that you can do it. More importantly, set plans and goals for your day that are achievable, and realistic.

Chapter 2: Why is Time Management So Important for Entrepreneurs?

As an entrepreneur, you consistently take risks and make decisions that affect a lot of people. You do all this with a bigger purpose: to succeed. For those who manage a large workforce, you have to deal with and manage time for a lot of people. This is one reason why time management should be an essential part of your life.

More often you come across people making excuses for not making it on time or completing tasks on time, or perhaps the job was too difficult for them to handle within the given timeframe. Why does this happen? As an entrepreneur, you cannot afford the luxury of wasting time. Once you spend time, you can never earn it back.

There are so many ways of managing time in your life as an entrepreneur. This is a factor that, when managed efficiently, can make the difference between success and failure. Today some programs are specifically designed to help you manage time better and manage your staff better. Given all the effort that is put in place to manage time, have you ever wondered why time management is crucial for you as an entrepreneur? Other than the apparent success-driven approach, here are some reasons why you should learn to manage your time:

Improved Decision Making

Whether you are getting help from one of your managers, or you have a list of things that you need to accomplish and cross off your own list, time management helps you with decision making. You become a better decision maker when you are in control of your time.

If you do not have sufficient time, you find yourself in a situation where you constantly have to make a rash decision without thinking it through. This is not good for your business. You make hasty decisions on gut feelings, and there is not much thought involved. You can make an awful choice in a split second, and regret it later on.

Managing your time allows you sufficient room to think clearly, weigh your options, and make the right move. You will avoid jumping to conclusions and making decisions out of poor judgment. Making the right call at the right time can make or break your career as an entrepreneur. Therefore, learn to manage your time well, and leave decision making to moments when you think clearly, if possible.

Proper time management also eases the pressure off you. You do not end up feeling you have a short amount of time to make a decision or to complete a given task. You are entirely in control, your body is well relaxed, and you can revel in the choices you make.

Stress Relief

One of the challenges behind struggling to accomplish so much in a short time is that your body is under undue pressure. The strain gets to you, and before long, this affects your health. A lot of entrepreneurs struggle with this. They take on too much for their bodies to handle and it never ends well.

Of what use is all your hard work and success if you have to spend all that money on medical bills? You need to enjoy your success. Your family needs to appreciate the person you have become. It all starts with time management.

Managing your time well means that you will have a lot of time on your hands to spend with those who matter. You have enough time to relax, take a walk, exercise, immerse yourself in the lives of the people who matter, without feeling pressured to do so.

How many entrepreneurs have you come across or read about who gained quite a fortune in their endeavors, but have always struggled to find peace when it comes to personal relations, even with their families? These are things you cannot take for granted, and it is in your best interest not to.

Staying in control of your time means you barely have to worry about stress. You will not feel rushed. You will not be overwhelmed by some of the tasks you have to accomplish. You will free yourself from the bondage of straining each day, and you will meet your deadlines.

Working Smart

One thing you notice with entrepreneurs who have made it in life is that they barely work hard. Instead, they work smart. This is not just one of those phrases thrown around to inspire people into entrepreneurship; it is a reality.

Managing time properly allows you a lot of room to focus, think about what you want to do and how to go about it. In time, you will learn how to do so much within a short period. How is this possible? You can address this in many ways. One that most entrepreneurs understand so well is to delegate duties. Choose the right person for the job, and you will have it completed faster, and efficiently.

When you have people doing things to make things work for you, you get the momentum to keep going. You see things working around you, and deep down you know you have the right people working with you. So, what do you do with the additional time earned from this?

You could think of ways to expand into other ventures. You might look into scaling up your operations. The time you have gained by delegating duties to others can be used for other things. You can also choose to refine your entrepreneurial skills or leadership prowess by enrolling in a class to learn something new.

Limited Resource

Time is limited, and however much you try to utilize it, you can never really have all the time you need in the world. Time is like a cake. Whichever way you want to slice it, it will always run out. To succeed in life as an entrepreneur, you must find a way to make the most use of the time you have. Get the right fit for your time.

You will come across those who either whine about how little time they have or brag about how much time they have. None of these tendencies will ever make a difference in your life. Instead, do something about the time *you* currently have.

You need to be a forward thinker. You need to be looking at ways of effectively managing your time. Forward thinking will go a long way towards helping you build an incredible venture. No one can stop you if you have your sights set on the right things, and can apportion your time accordingly.

Acquired Discipline

Time management is one of the aspects of self-discipline that all entrepreneurs tend to be good at. You value your time, and cannot afford to waste it. It follows that you can easily tell when someone is wasting your time or are about to. These are some of the interactions that you get rid of as soon as you can.

If you manage your time well, you learn to discipline yourself, and things will always seem to fall in place for you. These are essential skills that, over time, will make a big difference in your life, and help you achieve your goals faster.

Achieve Success

There are so many lists you might have come across highlighting some of the top personnel in your industry. You will stumble upon lists like Top 40 Under 40 and wonder how these fellows got so far in life. Well, amongst other things, they are very good at time management.

Time management and success go hand in hand. Take time and read about those who make it onto these lists and you will realize that none of them is excelling only at one thing. These are people who seem to have success all around them. They are heavily invested in different ventures and are doing equally well in all of them.

So, how do they manage to achieve it all? Amongst other reasons they will give, time management will be the common denominator. Staying in control of your time allows you to be in charge and monitor how things work around you. It is much better than letting things set their course. As an entrepreneur, you should map your course.

Control your destiny.

With each day passing day, you make better decisions, you are in control, and people keep noticing you make money moves. Being in control is how you end up on such lists of successful people. What's more, you will soon start attracting leaders, and other visionaries who are interested in learning how you are getting things done. Endorsements and deals might suddenly follow you.

You get an exposure that most people would kill for. You wake up in one city, have breakfast in another, lunch in another and dinner in another, all in one day. None of these things are achievable without proper time management.

Growth Opportunities

You are a beacon that guides your employees, or your partners. These are people who have probably seen you grow from strength to strength. They have seen you build your company from the ground up, and can always tell your story to everyone they come across with a bright smile and nothing but admiration.

The things you do, the way you go about your day, the

way you handle tasks, meetings, your interactions with the people around you, these are the things that matter. People will want to learn from you. They will want to get a seat at your table.

Through effective time management, you achieve so much that people have nothing but respect for you. When your peers and employees look up to you, this inspires them to become better. They also want to succeed in life just as much as you have. It fosters a sense of growth in them, and you will even notice the potential in them as they grow, nurture them, and hopefully champion them into better leaders.

What this means is that, through time management, you can inspire a generation. You can lift people out of their predicament and make them better versions of themselves. You can change lives, inspire change in communities, and make lives better. Unbeknownst to you, you will have left an impact on people's lives. There are people around you who will forever be grateful you came along their path in life.

Chapter 3: The Problem of Multitasking

It is amazing how many people try to multitask, attempt to squeeze a lot of things into a very short amount of time. More often than not, multitasking will be considered something of a superhero move. Those who seem to have perfected the art feel invincible. However, multitasking is not a good idea. It might work out for you from time to time, but you might end up doing more harm than good.

Many are the times you have envied those who multitask, perhaps because you are unable to. You can barely keep yourself together when struggling with one task, now imagine having to add another one. Truthfully, you have no business worrying about your inability to multitask. If you are multitasking, *you* should be worried.

Multitasking can easily interfere with your level of productivity. What you should be doing right now is figuring out how to stop it altogether and prioritize things.

Is It Really Working?

You seem to be completing all your tasks. You probably think multitasking is working for you, but in the real sense, it is not. You cannot rush some activities. A good testament of why you should stop multitasking is to consider a scenario where you are in a social place. Different people are trying to interact with you, resulting in you having conversations all over the place.

While all these conversations might be interesting, you can barely focus on them because your brain does not work that way. The brain is wired to focus on one thing at a time. Therefore, if you try to interact with one person, the brain automatically sets the former conversation on the back burner. This is why if you hold the new conversation a few seconds or minutes longer, you will turn back and realize that the person you were holding the recent conversation with might have lost interest or moved on to other things.

When you multitask, you get an illusion of mastery in whatever it is you are trying to achieve. However, in the long run, what it does successfully is take away your attention from the things that matter. You give half the attention you should be offering, and this never ends well.

Hinders Creativity

Studies into creativity have often revealed marvels about exploration and time. The brain needs a sufficient amount of time to process something and perfect it. If you keep jumping from one thing to the other, it becomes difficult for your brain to spend quality time getting used to something.

For an entrepreneur, creativity is one of the things you hold dear. This is how you come up with the ideas that have made you into the person you are. In case you find yourself constantly needing to multitask, you need to rethink your strategies.

You cannot be rushing things all over the place. You are not saving enough time for the things that matter. You cannot innovate anymore. If you try, you feel tired and bored and do not have that desire and drive to bring new ideas to life anymore. When you start multitasking, your ultimate goal is to get things done. Your concern is not about how to get them done, or the quality, but getting across the finish line. You might even end up missing so many excellent opportunities just because you were unable to focus on the things that matter.

Increased Stress

Imagine how good you usually feel when you have managed to complete one task. Imagine the strain it has on your body and the relief you have right after that. At the end of an important assignment, it is obvious you will feel spent. You will need to rejuvenate. If you are working on so many things at the same time, it becomes difficult for you to enjoy these moments.

Immediately, you are through with one task and you have to get onto another, and so forth. At times you have to complete so many tasks at the same time, and it becomes a risky situation for you. The stress that comes with multitasking can wear you down.

You will struggle to see your progress clearly over time. Other people might see it, but after a while, you might even end up losing the passion you once had for your venture. You might barely see the point anymore.

Multitasking takes its toll on your body, and you will struggle to replenish the resources it consumes from you each time. As time goes by, you feel worn out quickly, you strive to achieve results, you can barely spare the time to interact with family and friends, there is just so much going on around you, and you cannot cope. The level of stress that multitasking imposes on you is not something you would wish on anyone.

Damage to Your Brain

When multitasking, you might feel you are doing better, while in the real sense you are only succeeding at damaging your brain. Studies into multitasking reveal that those who often multitask tend to experience a reduction in the brain cells that regulate emotions, motivation, and cognitive control.

You might also develop memory problems. You end up struggling to recall information over a prolonged term. This happens both for long-term memory and for working memory too. This also explains why a lot of entrepreneurs who tend to multitask will not be passionate about what they once were, just a few months or years down the line. You do not have the same desire to succeed anymore. What you once loved has become mundane, and you no longer have the same interest you had in it earlier.

Distraction, Depression, and Anxiety

Based on scientific research, those who multitask often

end up being easy to distract. The distraction happens because the brain is so accustomed to interference that it becomes difficult for it to tell the difference between an important and a useless interruption.

If you are looking at productivity, over the long term, you are hurting yourself in ways you cannot imagine. The toll this will take on you is not worth the risk. You have to be at your best to meet the goals and objectives that you set out to achieve each day.

There is always that constant worry of whether or not you are good enough, whether you are doing things the right way, whether you are making the right steps, whether you will finish on time, and so forth. If you multitask often, you end up in a situation where you are always worried. You are always under pressure, under undue stress, and your brain grows accustomed to this. Anxiety and depression become your new normal.

You cannot keep pushing and punishing yourself like that. You have to find a way to stop multitasking. You have to learn to create and work within your schedules. Have a plan for your day and stick to it. Check things off your list one by one until you are through.

What to Do About Multitasking

While we have mentioned so many reasons why multitasking is not good for you, it is only fair that we also present a solution. More often than not, those who end up multitasking struggle with time management. This is why they are unable to do what they should at the right time, and end up squeezing everything together.

Before you get rid of multitasking, you must first understand why you are doing it. How are you losing time? Why are you lagging so much that you have to bundle everything together? Understand the challenges you are facing, how they manifest, and this will help you to overcome this problem.

The following are some simple changes that you can make in your routine to help you manage your time well, and help you stop multitasking:

Meaningless Interruptions – Know your worth. Know what is essential and what is not. Know your real purpose, so you can snap out of interactions that do not add value to your life at the moment. In the standard work scenario, there is always someone trying to get your attention, or something that is craving your attention, but in the real sense, you do not need to give it to them. These are the things that steal your time and force you to multitask.

Do away with distractions – The most obvious distraction most people are struggling with at the moment comes in the form of notifications. There are so many of these to handle. At work, turn off notifications. Do the same even when you are not at work, but need some peace. You do not need to attend to or address some of these things right away. You can deal with them later on.

Learn to say NO! – How many times have you heard this, but still did nothing about it? More often you are afraid to say no because you worry there might be repercussions. As it turns out, at times all you need is a No!. You have a set of priorities that you must meet, and if something or someone is presenting an obstacle to this, politely decline.

Scheduling Mix – While we are trying to do away with multitasking, it might not always be easy. There are instances when you might need to do more than one thing at a time. In such situations, you need to find the right scheduling mix for your activities. Allocate time when you are still fresh for the challenging tasks, so you can get them done without straining.

Chapter 4: Why You Cannot Get Anything Done?

You are struggling to clear things off your list, and you cannot seem to figure out why this is happening. One possible reason is procrastination. You seem to be putting things off until a later time when you can deal with them, but this is not working well for you either. You end up with piles of work, schedules uncleared, and before long people can barely trust you to get anything done.

This is a serious concern because it affects your confidence. It can break you down and make you feel weak and powerless. To deal with any problem, it is always wise to understand it and understand why you are having the problem in the first place. How does this problem arise? What is it in your environment that makes it easier for this problem to persist? How do you make a difference? A careful look at your day and schedule can reveal so much about some of the challenges you are struggling with. The following reasons might explain why you are unable to get things done.

You Love to Multitask

It is insane how a lot of people tend to thump their chests about how well they can multitask. While you can get things done, there is nothing much to write home about when it comes to multitasking. Multitasking is a vice you need to get rid of if you are to be as productive as you should be.

The information age has a lot of distortion in data access. You have to handle so much at the same time, and more often, you can barely hold down the fort. There is this obsession that people have with getting everything done to the point where they hardly take a moment to think about whether it is more efficient to handle things one at a time.

Think about this for a moment – How productive do you think you will be if you have to be on the phone with one of your clients, while at the same time you are trying to get some mathematical formula right on your Excel sheet? The chances are high neither of these will get the attention they deserve. You might mess up with the formula or fail to give the client the attention they need or deserve. You can even fail at both.

What if you paused your work on the Excel sheet,

listened to your client, addressed their needs, and then got back to your Excel sheet? The results will be different. Multitasking creates an element of distraction, and the more you get used to it, the more your concentration span goes down the drain.

This is one reason why you are barely getting things done, because at the end of the day, you are either too tired from overworking your brain, or you have a lot of things to clear. You end up with so many tasks that are *almost* complete.

It Is Not My Fault

There is more than enough blame going around in any workplace you visit. Someone is always pointing the finger at someone else. Very few people bother to own up and take responsibility for their actions.

One thing that blame does so well is that it steals time. It is like procrastination. The blame game often ends up in a heated exchange of words, or some form of go-slow while someone tries to understand why they are being forced to take responsibility for something that is not their fault.

Blaming others also affects productivity. It affects self-confidence. Blaming people for things that are not their fault essentially makes them feel like they are not good enough when, in the real sense, they are not the problem.

Let's say someone has earned a promotion ahead of you. Instead of being happy for them, you take this as an opportunity to find every reason to reprimand them. You talk ill of them behind their back. This is a time wastage, time that should be applied elsewhere.

You do realize that nothing comes of gossip, right? By the end of the day, this person will still be in the position they have earned. You will have lost a lot of time focusing on them. You might not be a sore loser, but instances like these make you look like one. It becomes a problem in the future because you might need the people you are talking ill of at the moment to support your cause for advancement up the career ladder.

Giving in to Distractions

Distractions are all over the place. Whether you allow them to manifest or not, is all up to you. A lot of people always complain about being distracted. However, it is essential to understand that distractions only take away your time if and when you allow them to.

No one can hold a gun to your head, forcing a distraction upon you. You are responsible for allowing the stimuli that are distracting you to replicate. You have full control of your time, but allow the distraction to take over when you respond to it.

Take the example of responding to your messages or emails at work. There is no pressure to do so. Unless you are expecting an urgent email or message that has to be responded to immediately, you are under no pressure to respond as they stream into your device. When you do, you allow yourself to be distracted.

There is, however, a way around this. Turn off the notifications on your phone. Put your phone on silent mode. Turn off pop-ups from your laptop. These are things that will overwhelm you, distract you from the things that matter, yet you have the power to take back control.

At times you have to take personal responsibility for your actions. Distractions do not force their way into your life. They present their case, and you allow them in. Stop allowing distractions to control your life, and you will have more time to complete your tasks.

Daydreaming

Daydreaming is one of the other reasons why you are not getting things done. You spend a lot of time thinking, thinking about so much, but doing nothing about it. Let's say you are thinking of something credible and constructive. Can you do something about it? Can you act on it and make it happen immediately? If this is not the case, spare yourself the trauma, and get some work done.

Planning is an essential part of success. However, you cannot plan for the rest of your life. Make plans and act on them. Do not make plans and keep pushing them aside. If you do not work on the plan, it will end up being nothing but a dream. Actualize your plans. Be proactive. Do not think and then do very little about the things you were thinking about.

Obsession

There is nothing wrong with wanting the good things in life. It is only reasonable that you do. Everyone wants to wake up in a better position tomorrow than they were today. However, you should know the difference between wanting the best for yourself and obsession.

The problem with obsession is that you spend a lot of time thinking about things that you do not have any control over. This raises a lot of challenges for you, especially regarding time wasted. It can easily lead you into the daydreaming trap, whereby you become distracted by the slightest thought of something that you have been obsessing about.

In the long run, you might be left with nothing but regret and stress, especially when you realize you cannot get the things you have been stressing about.

Inability to Say NO

This does not come as a surprise. In the workplace, if you are the person who can never say no to anyone, you will end up with a lot of work on your table. You will end up doing the work that is not supposed to be yours in the first place.

When will you ever get your work done if you are continually working hard to complete tasks for other people? The thing about this inability to say no is that it comes at a price. If you cannot say no, it is evident that you will also have to struggle to impress.

When you offer to do something for someone because they seemingly asked you politely, you try to do it correctly so that they are impressed. You try to maintain this good image in their ranks so that they see the good in you.

There is nothing wrong with helping people. Feel free to assist whenever you can. However, how can you help someone when you can barely support yourself? At the risk of being self-centered, you must learn to put yourself first.

In the corporate world today, everyone seems to focus on themselves. The attention is on what works for them, what is right for them. The sooner you realize that people will often want to use you as a stepping stone to achieve their own targets, the easier it will be for you to set and get your priorities right.

Self-Improvement, or Not!

For you to be in this position, where you are wondering why you are unable to get things done, you have probably found yourself at the wrong end of your schedules many times. Today there are so many self-improvement articles, books, and even webinars that you can use to help you overcome some of these challenges. Thanks to the internet, help is not always far away.

However, as many people do, you have access to some quality support, but you do nothing about it. You have read so many books, articles, blog posts on time management, procrastination, organizing yourself at work, and so forth. You can quote more than ten phrases from the materials you have come across off the top of your head. The problem is that, even with all this material, you are doing nothing about changing your predicament.

You still find yourself stuck in the rat race that is disorganization. You still struggle to get things done, and at the end of the day, you still have work spilling over into a new day. What gives? You have to start putting into practice the things you learn. You might not be able to address all of them at the same time, but take small steps towards improving your situation.

It takes a lot of will and initiative for you to make the bold step and make the changes you want. Success never comes easy – let no one lie to you about that. Self-improvement and empowerment are a result of a personal initiative. You commit to doing things differently. You make a personal commitment to planning your day and working according to your schedules. What we are getting at is the fact that you already have the answers you are looking for.

The champion you are struggling to become already lies within you. You merely need to realize this and unleash your champion. Give them a purpose and let your champion fight for you. Remember, you are only ever going to be as good and strong as your will to challenge yourself from holding yourself back. No one else can!

Chapter 5: Where Did Your Time Go?

At the end of the day, many people struggle to understand how time went by so fast. You wake up in the morning ready for a beautiful day ahead. A short while later, the day is over, and you can barely remember where the time went. This happens so often, the struggle to account for lost time.

There are several reasons why you lose time or lose track of time, and fail to understand what happened. These are simple things that you do out of habit to the point where they become part and parcel of your routine. Like corruption, some of these elements become institutionalized to the point where you can barely tell when you are losing time.

The first step towards getting back control is to understand where you lose time, and how. This explains why most people struggle to meet their deadlines or complete tasks on time. Examine yourself carefully, and you will notice how some of these elements manifest.

The only thing holding you back from realizing your true potential is yourself. Proper time management involves improving on some of your time-wasting challenges. In case you are still not sure where your time goes, here are some of the common ways you could be losing time each day.

Disorganization

Instead of working on your priority tasks, you find yourself spending a lot of time trying to find people or documents, trying to trace emails, make calls, make follow-ups. If you are often lagging, or struggling to keep up the pace with your colleagues, there is a good chance you are disorganized. Unfortunately, some people are so disorganized in a very organized manner, and they can barely tell the difference.

Do not waste time with mundane tasks. Prepare adequately for the day ahead. Get in ahead of time. Starting your day early will help with this. Since you are at your desk earlier, you have enough time to prepare, organize the desk, look at your schedule and plan out your work for the rest of the day.

You have a lot of items to check off your list, so create a priority list or order of handling your work for the day.

This list will not just help you be on the same page with your workmates, but it will also help you become more efficient, and improve your overall contribution to the team. Do not play catch-up anymore. Get your head right in the game!

Gossip

You would be surprised how many times people gossip about others and go about their business like nothing has happened. The problem with gossip is that it takes up a lot of your time, and before you know it, the day is gone.

The juicier the story, the more time it will cost you. Talking about people behind their back does not make you a better person than they are. Having some of the information you seek so keenly might not even do you any good in the long run. You will do so much better spending more time on your tasks than gossiping.

The other problem with gossiping is that, the more you talk to someone about someone else, the higher the chances they will have something to say to someone else about you. Gossip creates a vicious cycle that never ends, and creates an element of hatred in your own circle.

Anxiety and Worry

Let's face it, there are times when worry and anxiety are a part of your day, brought on by events beyond your control. In such cases, it would be wise to seek help from the relevant persons. However, apart from exceptional circumstances, worry is nothing but a waste of your energy – good energy to be precise!

If you find yourself worrying about something, do not sit on it – be proactive and act on it. Talk to someone, do something. As long as the object of your concern is not on your plate anymore, it becomes someone else's concern and allows you to sharpen your focus and think about other things.

Nothing eats up more of your time than sitting down and worrying about something that you can do nothing about. Spare that energy and use it on something more constructive, and you might end up with more time on your hands at the end of the day.

Emails

Emails have made communication easier, better, and more convenient. However, they can become a distraction. A lot of people check and respond to their emails instantly. While this might be a good idea, because it helps you keep a clean email and reduces strain, it is also counterproductive.

You can easily spend most of your day checking, sending, and responding to emails, and before you know it, you might move on to other things. So, what should you do about this? First, set aside specific times during the day when you can tend to your emails. Deal with all your emails at this time. Unless you have an urgent email to deal with, stay away from your emails outside your set email time.

Procrastination

Time wasted will never be earned back. This is something you have to realize with procrastination. You lose a lot of time because you do not want to handle something when you could have already completed it all together, and instead spend time on something else.

Procrastination is common, not just at work, but in all aspects of your life. There are things you know you should do, but for some reason you find comfort in putting them off just a while longer while you focus on something else that supposedly gives you more satisfaction.

Perhaps you do not want to handle something immediately, or maybe you are just afraid to get it done. The sooner you can start doing something, the sooner you will have it completed and free up time to do whatever you please.

Procrastination is a habitual vice. If it has already manifested in your life, you should also make a habit of doing things and getting them done. Get in the habit of completing tasks as and when they are supposed to be done. This will gain you a lot of time over the course of your day.

Keeping Up with News

There is always something happening somewhere, something you are interested in. Different news items might get your attention. Information is an attention industry. The information providers are spending lots of money by the minute to mine data about you, and they use this to send you news items that interest you.

If you are a sports person, they will trawl your internet usage and learn more about the teams you are interested in. Therefore, more and more information sources will come your way. It is very easy to become a slave to the 24/7 news industry.

Something will always get your attention. If it is not an analysis of your favorite team playing poorly over the weekend, it is something about a new study that touches something you are passionate about. It could also be a piece about a new trick that might help you save on fuel when you are driving your car, or how to get the attention of your crush.

The more time you spend reading the news, the more time you will lose in your day. Unfortunately, most news providers these days use all methods possible to get your attention, even resorting to tactics that were often common with the gutter press. While you spend a lot of time reading about the latest scandals in government, a bigger scandal will be brewing in your personal space – the scandal of hours lost without any returns.

Social Media

Social media ranks highly on the list of time usurpers. It is by far one of the most efficient ways of wasting time. The moment you open your Twitter account, you will come across exciting stuff and, before you know it, the day is gone. Many are those who have admittedly opened their Twitter app on their phone at 10pm, hoping to spend a few minutes on the phone, then fall asleep, only to realize it is 3am and the only thing sending them to sleep is the battery running low.

Take YouTube as another good example. You check in to watch this video link a close friend sent you about making waffles. 3 hours later, you are watching cats babysitting, and cannot understand how you found yourself in this predicament.

Put your phone away. If you are on your laptop, stay away from social media networks. There are tools today that you can install which block social media access at periods when you are busy with other things. These will help you to become more productive.

Remember, however, that it takes a lot of willpower to do this. After all, you can always turn off the tools and keep up with that rant on Twitter that's got everyone talking. If you are taking a break from work, stay away from your phone too. Take a walk, talk to someone, get some fresh air, have some juice. Do something else other than burying your head in social media.

Toxic Relationships

Everyone has been in this situation at some point. Toxic relationships not only waste your time, they waste your life. You lose a part of yourself to some of these relationships. They change you. It is not just about personal relationships; it also applies to relationships at work, with colleagues or clients.

You have clients who demand so much but pay very little or nothing at all. Why do you still keep them around? The only thing this does is drain you, emotionally and psychologically. After a while, you will be physically exhausted too.

You should learn to value yourself, and your time. Value addition is important. You should not focus your efforts on delivering value while you receive none in return. Value addition is a quid pro quo situation.

Take your time and monitor how you interact with different clients. You will realize that you spend more time with and for those who appreciate your effort. These are clients who do not just see you as a means to an end, a tool, but as a person, an important one, to be precise. Anyone who does not value you right now will probably never appreciate you. You might end up putting in a lot of work to justify yourself, your position, your presence, yet you didn't even matter in the first place.

Appreciate yourself, appreciate your time, strive to get value for your presence and existence, and cut off relationships that are toxic.

Taking Shortcuts

Everyone uses shortcuts at some point. From repurposing, copy-pasting, plagiarizing, there are so many ways. Instead of talking to someone directly, you use someone else to get you there. It would have been much faster, easier, and more direct if you approached them on your own.

While some shortcuts are useful, they are not the best way to go about your day. You will lose a lot of time in the process. If you succeed, you form a habit of using shortcuts. Eventually, you get caught.

The problem with shortcuts is that, not only do they waste your time in an attempt to save time, but you might lose clients, damage relationships, and so forth. Try to be more direct in your engagements, and you will never have to struggle to account for your time.

Chapter 6: Time Saving Strategies

Time is a resource that cannot be recovered once it is spent. You have minimal time within which you need to accomplish a lot of tasks. What you can do, however, is change the way you spend your time.

You know so many executives who put in more than 50 hours a week and still manage to spend time with their families and take holidays. You also know people who work 30 hours a week and complain about how they do not have enough time to spend with their families. What is the difference between these two sets of people? In which category do you fall?

The difference is time management, and setting priorities. One of these groups understands what is essential, while the other doesn't. The secret to time management is realizing how much time you have, and what you can do with it. Some people even plan for the time they know they do not have. They plan for other people's time, and effectively make it theirs. This is what executives do, and that is how they are able to take time off to have fun.

What lesson can you learn from executives about managing other people's time? If you cannot control your time, someone else will manage it for you. This is a common phrase that you might have come across in so many places, but it is true. This is what most managers do. They have their eyes on the bigger picture. They have plans on how to get there. They have their ideas for their own time.

Before they whisk away to meetings, they make sure they have their teams fully engaged. As they are busy in discussions and making presentations, people are busy working on their agenda. A task that would take five people 6 hours can be completed much earlier, by adding one or two more people to that group. That is how they save time.

Therefore, it is all about maximizing the time that you have. Never spend your energy worrying about time that you do not have. If someone else has it, and you can manage it and make it yours like managers do, go right ahead and do it.

How do you optimize your time? How do you make sure each hour is put to good use? Here are some useful tips that can help you:

Tracking Your Time

You would be surprised by how many people track their time – very few. Most people go about their day haphazardly. Get into the habit of accounting for your time. Like money, time is precious, and you need to know where and how you spend it. That way, when you find yourself going broke, you can trace your steps and find out where all the money went.

Have a plan to track your time from the moment you wake up to the time you go to sleep. If this is new to you, do not rush it, give it a try for a week or two. Write down the things you do, how much time you spend on each activity. Write down how much time you spend on breaks.

By taking note of these simple things, you can sit down at the end of the week and evaluate how you spent your work week. Time tracking is an exercise that might seem so simple, but it has far-reaching effects. Imagine someone spends more than 30 minutes each morning just trying to figure out what they want to wear that day. Someone else spends 15 of that 30 minutes writing down their plan for their day, and by the end of the 30 minutes, they will have also completed 15 minutes of meditation. Who between these two will have a productive morning?

When you review your timestamps, you might be surprised at how much time you have been wasting. Now keep that experiment up for a whole month, then group similar and recurring tasks. Do the math and see how much time you are spending on productive tasks, how much time you are spending on breaks, how much time you are using on non-important things during your productive hours. You should also highlight how much time you waste in the mornings when you are full of energy.

Establish a Hierarchy of Tasks

Carefully look at the tasks you need to accomplish. Which are the optional ones and which are the important ones? How often do you go about your work without making a distinction between the two?

Having figured this out, reschedule your days around the critical tasks. Slot them in early in the morning. You are still fresh and full of energy at this hour. It is the right time to start working on challenging tasks. Anything else can be done later on in the day.

A big mistake that most people make is to start their day

with easy tasks or go about their day without a plan altogether. This is the easiest way to become distracted. Besides, if you start working on the easy ones, later on, when you try to work on the difficult tasks, your brain might not be as cooperative as it would have been in the morning. This is also a good window of opportunity for procrastination.

Decluttering your desk will also help you to save time. This is the time that you would have wasted looking for something that is probably not on your desk or concealed by files. A disorganized desk is an easy way of getting distracted.

Start Your Day Early

Do you know you can earn yourself more than an hour each week by waking up 30 minutes earlier than you often do? This is 30 minutes that you can use for so many things. Since it is too early in the morning, and no one will disturb you with calls, you can send and respond to emails. You can also use this time for exercise.

Internet Usage

The internet is all over the place these days. You either have your device connected to a data service provider, or you are using the office or home wireless internet. A lot of the things you do today require internet access for research.

While the internet is important to your work, you do not have to be online all the time. Having completed your research, you can go offline and get your work done. Let's say you are a creative writer. Save the pages you need, download the documents you need for research, and go offline. Work on your notes and organize your thoughts, then write the piece you need to.

Staying online will see you lose track of time. Information overload affects a lot of people these days. The people who run media houses and news centers all over the world have taken time to study the mannerisms of their consumers. They know the times when people are more active, the times when people seem to consume more content from their websites. These are the times when they churn out titles that they know will get your attention.

It is easy to get sucked into this abyss, and once you are

in, there is no coming back. The websites will have received traffic from your end, but at the expense of your work, and your time. Think about this: how many times have you gone online to read the news or check a flight schedule, yet a few minutes later you find yourself still online but reading something else not related to the first thing you were looking for online? The secret is to set time aside for internet access and respect it. You can even block your browser from accessing certain websites during your busy schedule, especially social media websites.

Managing Expectations

Can you really do what you want to? Do you have enough time in your schedule to squeeze it in? While it is good to make plans, try not to be too ambitious. The only thing you will have managed to do is plan to fail. Keep your plans reasonable. There are things that you know you cannot do, so do not lie to yourself.

Here's a good example. Let's say you have noticed you have a lot of things to do, and you are trying to make use of your mornings. You decide to slot a gym session, preparing your children for school, laundry, and walk the dog, all before 9am. This is preposterous. One or two of these tasks will not be done, or will not receive the attention they deserve. By 9am, if you manage to do all this, you will be too exhausted, you might have to take more time to rest.

Instead of biting off more than you can chew, you can delegate some of these tasks. Have someone walk the dog, and someone else doing laundry. Space out your tasks accordingly. It makes your list realistic, and achievable.

Grouping Tasks

You can save a lot of time when you group some tasks. This is a lesson a lot of people learn when they buy their first car, for example. As you make plans to buy the car, you think about how you will be driving wherever you want to go. It is evident because of the excitement. You want to get a good feel of the car. You need to feel good about owning the car.

However, after a while, you realize you are wasting fuel. You cannot be driving everywhere. You cannot be the designated driver for everyone. You soon realize you cannot keep going out of your way to pick people up, and more importantly, you recognize the need to group tasks. You look at your list for things that are missing in the house, and you create a map in your mind of how you can pick all of them up in one trip without going back and forth. Suddenly, it makes sense to leave the car at home some days.

This is the same concept you need to introduce into your day. Look at the things you need to accomplish. How many of the tasks are similar? How many of them will require you to be in the same place? You can group those so that, when you go to that place, you do many things at once.

If you are at the office, how many tasks need you to be on the 7th and 8th floor? Group those tasks if you can. This way, you can leave your office, attend to them, and come back. You will have saved yourself unnecessary trips in and out of your office.

Set aside time to make calls or answer emails. This is better than responding to every email as soon as they hit your inbox, or making calls every 10 minutes. You might not be able to focus on anything else. You do not want to look like a busybody. You will also save so much time in the process.

Your Work Schedule

What kind of schedule do you have? How much control do you have over it? Is it so flexible you can choose your work hours? If possible, make sure you adjust your hours accordingly. Get things done within the set timeframe. If you have an 8-hour shift, try to get as much work done during the early hours of your shift. Try to spend at least 6 of those hours being productive. You do not need to exert a lot of strain to deliver results.

When you prioritize your tasks, you save a lot of time in the process. You end up wasting very little time. If you are unable to choose your work hours, work with what you have and make the most of it.

Consider your commute. The more challenging your commute to work is, the higher the chance that your first hour at work might not be productive. Your body needs to adjust to the trauma of the commute. If you do not commute through peak hours, you can get a lot of work done when most people have left the office.

You can also talk to your superior about restructuring or reprioritizing your work. Talk to them about the new changes you are making in your life. Tell your boss you want to be more effective, and the plan you have for your day. Together, you can work out how to get things done. They can also act as your mentor, especially when you are just starting to work on this time-saving plan. It is something you would have done on your own, but by discussing it with your boss, you are bringing in someone to keep you in check, someone that you will be answerable to. It will help you learn some discipline about the new strategy.

Meetings and Conversations

You might know this already – not all meetings at work are productive. You have probably attended so many of them you know which ones you can skip without any repercussions. Spending a lot of time in meetings only eats up the time you should be doing something else. There is no need to attend a meeting and listen to people talk about things that they could have sent in an email. Get out of such meetings. If necessary, you can send a junior representative to take notes and brief you. While some of these meetings are going on, the movement in the office reduces, and you can complete a lot of work without distraction.

While it is okay to talk to your workmates, holding long conversations is a waste of time. These conversations have nothing to do with the work you are supposed to do. It might be gossip, or you might be catching up, especially with the person who sits next to you. These conversations give the illusion of maintaining good friendships and relationships. However, they also take away a lot of your time. Engage your peers, but know when to set limits to the conversation time. Besides, you can politely tell your colleague to tone it down a bit, so both of you can get some work going.

Chapter 7: Building a Rock-Solid Routine

It is easy to work through your day when you have a routine. The more you work with a routine, the more your body gets used to it, and it becomes a matter of habit. This is something that will get you through some of the toughest days of your life. Once you have worked out a routine, it is crucial that you maintain discipline going through it. Without restraint, it is impossible to make progress. You will continuously find reasons or excuses to do something else other than what is most important.

Tips for a Successful Routine

To create and maintain a successful routine, the following are some of the useful tips that should guide you:

Start Early

The earlier you start your day, the better it will be. Starting your day early means you have to sleep early too.

Waking up early will help you stay fresh and focused. You have a lot of time very early in the day to do as you please. You can take notes and compare how you perform on the days you wake up early, and the days you wake up late.

Quality Sleep

There is a good reason why you are advised to get quality sleep at night. Try to get your 7 or 8 hours. Quality sleep is vital for a lot of reasons. It is the time your body gets to rest. It is the time your organs are relaxed and rejuvenating. Your blood circulation will be better in the morning if you slept well.

You constantly put your body under pressure and strain as you try to maneuver through your deadlines, meetings, and other things you have to complete through the day. By the close of business, your energy is depleted, and your muscles are worn out. Besides, without proper sleep, any money you earn will be spent on medical expenses.

There are a lot of people who visit doctors complaining about all manner of symptoms, and upon examination, the doctor recommends bed rest. Imagine going to a doctor, only to be told you need to sleep better.

Exercise

However pressed you are for time, you are never too pressed to find time for exercise. When we talk about exercise, we do not necessarily mean trying to compete in the World's Strongest Human challenge. Something sensible will do.

You can schedule your exercise routines to suit your lifestyle. For exercise, you can do a few stretches, run a few kilometers in the morning, take a walk in the evening, do some sit-ups, or spend a few minutes on meditation and yoga. There are endless things you can do for exercise.

Since you are working on a routine, keep this up for a few days and you will notice how easily it becomes a regular part of your day. Exercise is an excellent way to strengthen your body, mentally and physically.

Get Some Alone Time

Getting alone time is something that people never used to take seriously. Today it is of utmost importance that you do so. This allows you to reflect upon your day, think about the future, make plans, or relax and while away time.

You can use this time for meditation. Some people do it

in the morning, others late in the evening. For some, they find time for it during a busy day, and it helps them rejuvenate and come back stronger. You can create a schedule that works just for you.

Meditation will help you take a break from the stress in your schedule, and overcome fatigue. Other than meditation, you can also read a book during your alone time. It is important that you pay attention to the material you read. You are primarily feeding your mind, so you must be keen on what you feed it. You do not necessarily need to read a paperback. You can find something on Kindle, or listen to an audiobook. Find something that adds value to your life, books that nourish your soul.

Importance of Milestones

You have a lot of things that you should get done by the end of the day. Since you cannot do it all at once, you should break things into manageable milestones. Milestones can be accomplished faster and easier. The more you achieve them, the more psyched up you will be to take on the next one.

Avoid Perfectionism

No one is perfect out there. Things will not always go according to plan. These are some of the facts that you should never forget. Even as you work on creating a routine, you must remember that you are not perfect.

There are some challenges that perfectionists struggle through. You might end up being uptight or alienating people around you. Give yourself enough time to do things, and do them correctly. Have a list that you can follow and work through. Be patient with yourself and those around you, especially if either of you is not having a perfect day. Everyone has one of those off days from time to time.

Discipline

One of the most important factors behind a successful routine is discipline. You need to learn to respect your routine enough to be disciplined in executing it. With discipline, you will also need to set time limits for what you are doing. Space things out accordingly. Do not force yourself to handle tasks in a timeframe that is virtually impossible to manage. If you have one of those bad days when things do not seem to be working, do not beat yourself up about it. Take a step back, and bounce back harder.

Creating the Routine

Having looked at some guiding tips on creating the perfect routine, here are the steps to follow when creating that routine:

Start with a List

Take your time to write a list of all the things you need to do in a day. There might not be a particular order; just make a list. Get your notepad ready and spend 15-30 minutes doing this. In case you are not sure how to identify the things you need to do, ask yourself some simple questions. It is the answers you need to note down.

Your list should include things like errands to be completed that day, things to do before or after taking kids to school, or things you agreed to do for your partner. Make a list of things to be done around the house when you are around or away, technicians who might be coming over to fix something, a meeting you have planned for the day, or a dinner reservation.

Remember that nothing is too small to be included on this list – including brushing your teeth. You can refine the list later on.

Establish a Schedule

Since you already have a list of things to do, you can now think about where to slot them into your day. Identify the tasks that demand a lot of energy. It is wise to have these very early in the day. If you need to do something that involves driving somewhere, factor in the traffic constraint, and allow yourself enough room for uncertainties.

A simple rule of thumb, always reserve your mornings for things that demand a lot of critical thinking. For creatives, this is the best time to get fresh ideas popping. As the day goes by, your coffee high should have already dissipated, and you might be more inclined to tackle routine or boring things.

This is the appropriate time for making appointments, taking meetings, and so forth. Besides, interacting with other people at this juncture will help you break the monotony that you might have in your morning schedule. Run your errands during this time too.

Evenings are supposed to be for slower, more relaxed

stuff. Declutter, play with the kids, pack your lunch for tomorrow, make plans for the next day, and so forth. Look at the list you had and make sure you have slotted in everything at the right time.

Flexibility

Even though you are working to a routine, you should remember to keep things flexible a bit. There are times when things might not always go according to plan, and it is okay. Try to work in some wiggle room into your program, as this will help you to take care of inconveniences and unforeseen circumstances. Having done that, you can start putting your list together. Match tasks with the right time and you will have the routine ready.

Evaluation

You have to evaluate the routine to see how effective it is. Try it out for a few days. Note any changes that you experience as you work around the routine. Is it making your life better? Do you have more time at the end of the day? Do you feel the routine is efficient?

You should note progress after a while, or any strain it might be causing you. If you are straining, go back to the drawing board and come up with a new plan, or make changes where necessary.

Importance of a Routine

Why is it essential for you to create a routine? What benefits will you gain from having one, that you never had when you did not have one?

Efficiency

A routine helps you become efficient in everything that you do. It enables you to reduce the time you spend on mundane or unnecessary things. With a routine, you know what to do, and when to do it, and manage your time correctly.

Focus

One thing that a routine does so well is help you to focus and get an element of structure in your life. You are more organized when you have a routine than when you do not have one. As you familiarize yourself with the routine, things become more comfortable for you.

Proper Planning

A routine helps you spend less time planning because you already know what to do and when to do it. You no longer have to make guesses on the day, but wake up knowing what you need to do.

Time Saver

Time is a valuable resource. With a routine, you succeed at time management. You have your day worked out efficiently, and this helps you to make the right decisions about how to use your time.

Habitual Concerns

Having a routine will help you drop some bad habits and start good ones. You are trying to reach your potential, so a routine will help you weed out some of the things that have been stealing your time, which are not important.

At the same time, you learn some useful traits like self-discipline when you have and follow a working routine. As you keep doing things, in the same way each day, they become part and parcel of who you are.

Accomplishment

Routines give you a sense of accomplishment. You wake up each day with a checklist of things to do. As you power through the day, striking stuff off your list one by one, you feel good about the day. You feel good about yourself too. You challenge yourself to accomplish more as time goes by.

Priorities

One of the benefits of using a routine is that you will learn the important things and how to slot them into your day. Over time, you will also learn a lot about yourself, and how your energy flows throughout the day. Soon it will be easier to schedule things on your to-do list without necessarily writing them down. This is because you know when you can free up time, and when you cannot afford distractions.

Chapter 8: Taming Your Tools

You have already figured out some of the important ways you can save time or make more use of your time. You probably have some tools in place that can guide you through it. The challenge, however, is how to tame these tools, how to use them effectively to help you become successful in your venture.

The thing about time is, you have very little of it to work with. Therefore, you cannot afford the luxury of doing things over and over. You should start doing things once and getting them right first time around. You should avoid instances where you have to repeat tasks because this never bodes well. You end up using the time that should have been set aside for something else. However busy you are, you can still make sure you give everything your best effort.

You have to increase your productivity in each task you take up. This allows you to perform more in the limited time you have. At the same time, try not to rush your work because no one pays for shoddy work. You might lose your contracts, or lose your job altogether.

What you need to do is find the right mixture of techniques and tools to help you become more productive. You have many tools that you can use to help you live an organized life. You must learn to block distractions from your busy time, set schedules that you can follow, and allow yourself enough time to rest.

The following is a guide on how to achieve the perfect mix. If you already have a system in place, you can use this to refine your system.

Choosing the Right Time Management System

The time management business is thriving, and rightly so. Today, many people have realized they are not making the most use of their time and, as a result, they look for options, tools to help them become more productive. There is nothing wrong with that. There is also nothing wrong with entrepreneurs who realize this need and do something about it. What you end up with, however, is a market where there are so many tools you are spoilt for choice.

Your time management skills might not be the best out there, but realizing this and admitting it is the first step towards a better future. Without proper planning, you might find yourself jumping from one crisis to another without getting time to refresh.

There are lots of systems that you can use to help you manage your time better. Do not jump the gun and pick the first system you come across. Take your time. Research, read, brainstorm, find out as much as you can about the tools you come across. At times all you need to do is be more organized. Have a look at the way you go about your day and change things around.

Have a to-do list. It might not be one of the most innovative suggestions, but it is something that can guide you on what you need to get done throughout the day. This list gives you structure and an order in which to do things. You can use a straightforward list, where you check things off one by one, or depending on the level of complexity of your schedules, you can find a more elaborate list. These days you have lists that you can share with a team in case you are collaborating on projects. This will also help you stay focused because there are a lot of people involved in the project you are working on.

Remember, just because a system works for someone you know does not necessarily mean it will work well for you. You must keep an open mind when going about this.

Organization

For any of the tools you are using to be effective, you have to understand how important the tasks at hand are. Organization is, in fact, one of the most important things. It will help you establish and organize your list of priorities. There is no use coming up with a list, only for you to push the difficult tasks to a later date, and instead spend most of your day working on simpler things. This level of procrastination will lead to your ruin in the long run.

Determine the critical tasks for the day. Tackle them as soon as possible. The earlier you get them out of the way, the sooner you can start working on simpler tasks, and free up time. You can also create categories for your work. Identify things that have to be completed by the end of the day, others that need to be completed over a certain period of time, and apportion your time for them accordingly.

However difficult or boring the tasks set for the morning are, try to power through them. This is the time you are at your best, and you have the energy to handle them accordingly.

Respect Your Productive Time

One of the first things you do when you wake up in the morning is find your phone and go through your emails or your social media accounts. You go through this until you have cleared all the notifications, or until you have something pressing to deal with. You might think it is fantastic being in the know, but in the real sense, you have started your day a distracted fellow.

Checking these platforms very early in the morning means your mind is already interested in some story that you have come across. After all, there is always something exciting happening on social media, something that piques your interest.

Social media companies spend a lot of money creating and refining their algorithms to make sure that they deliver content that is tailor-made to suit your needs. They trawl your account, the things you like, the conversations you have online, track the words you wish to use, and through their algorithms they use this to send you updates about things that can keep you hooked long enough.

Checking your emails or social media notifications is not supposed to be a top priority task, but unfortunately most people treat it as such. If you want to be and stay productive, create a time in the day when you check your emails, social media accounts, and respond to whatever needs your attention. The best time for this is in the afternoon. This is the time when most people are not attentive, people are bored, and the energy they had at the beginning of their day has dissipated.

Even as you do this, try not to spend a lot of time on it. Glancing at your phone for 5 minutes can quickly turn into an hour. Those notifications will not make a difference in your life whether you respond to them immediately or two hours later. So what if you miss out on some celebrity gossip? They are living their lives. What if you have not seen the banter going on about the game last weekend? It does not change the results, and might not even affect the results of the next game. Keep your head in the game.

Using the Right Planning Apps

There are so many apps that can help you manage your time properly and improve your productivity. These apps also help you manage your lists. You can type in projects that you need to handle by the end of the day. Split the projects into simple, manageable tasks if they are too big and set priority levels for every single task.

If you are working with a team, one of the best planning apps is Trello. It is ideal for creating the perfect vision for your projects. With Trello, you can assign members of your team tasks. You create boards that are a representation of the projects. In each of the boards, you can create a list of things to do, and cards that represent the tasks that are incomplete. This way, everyone has something in particular that they are working on, and they can also see what each other has to do. If someone is slacking, anyone in the group can nudge them to improve, so they do not lag the entire project behind.

Appreciate Your Breaks

Taking a break from work to relax is not bad. A break will help you become productive. You need to make sure you are disciplined enough not to take more time than you need. Your mind needs to get some rest, especially after concentrating on tasks, for the longest time possible. Your body, on the other hand, needs to rest.

It is while you are taking this breather that you might get some fresh ideas about how to handle the challenges you are having with your projects or your personal concerns. To make the most use of your breaks, get away from the workplace. If you can, take a few minutes' walk away from your office or cubicle.

If you cannot create these breaks, your mind will automatically find a way to create them and wander away when you are exhausted. It is not easy to come back from this, and even if you do, you might not be as productive as you should.

Free Yourself from the Digital World

If you find yourself struggling to focus, there is nothing wrong with taking a hiatus from the digital world. Many people have done it and succeeded. You can limit your communication to the simple things: making phone calls and checking office emails. Take a break from social media. Delete the apps from your phone. You can even temporarily close your account, or close it permanently.

You need time to get things running. You need time to focus and get control over your life. Do whatever it takes. In the long run, you will look back and appreciate the decision you made. Here's something interesting that most people might not be aware of – most, if not all of the people at the helm of tech companies in the world, strive to make sure they have a buffer zone in their homes. They have a place where there is no access to the internet, a place where no devices are allowed inside. These are places where they sit and relax with their families, free from the distractions from the rest of the world. You can do the same.

Taking Detailed Notes

Taking notes is one thing, taking detailed notes is another altogether. Adding valuable details in your notes makes it easier for you to follow up. You know what you were doing and what comes next. Detailed notes are important, especially when you are collaborating with someone on a task. It will also help you remember where to pick up from, especially if you haven't communicated with someone in a while.

Say, for example, you have sent someone an email. What next? In your to-do list where you have the notification to send emails, you can include a note that you are waiting to hear from them. This way, at the specified time of the day you have set aside to check your notes, you know you have an email to follow up on.

These are some of the simple things that will help you save time and make the most use of the tools you are using.

Chapter 9: Priorities and Goals

Priorities and goals determine your success or failure. Many people have goals and priorities, but they are skewed or misplaced. As a result, they end up failing, not because they did not know what to do, but because they did not know how to go about it. Even with the right idea, it is still possible to fail. The secret is learning the perfect balance and how to implement and enforce your goals and priorities.

Unfortunately, most people are not so good at setting their priorities or goals. It gets even worse when you are just starting your business. No manual comes with this. You need to make so many decisions, some of which are confusing, and you might not understand them well. As a result, you find yourself focusing on things that might feel right at the moment, but in hindsight, they were not supposed to receive the priority you gave them. This is how you end up losing track, and if unchecked, you might lose the desire to keep working on your project.

Your list of priorities should start with things that are important to you. You should realize that, while it is possible for you to do anything you want, it is impossible to do everything at the same time. When thinking about priorities, look at them in terms of timelines within which you need to achieve them. The following is a brief guide that will help you set your priorities straight.

What Is Important to You?

Whether you are thinking about priorities for yourself or your business, you have to know what you are working towards. What is important to you? What are the core activities you engage in, or those that your business engages in, that are important? Priorities should align with long-term goals and objectives.

It is through setting priorities and meeting them that you achieve your goals. It is almost impossible to reach your goals in the timelines you set if you do not follow your set priorities. Finding the correct answers to these questions will also help you to understand the decision-making process for your company or understand what you need to do as an individual to make things better in your life.

In the workplace, it is very easy to become overrun by things that do not matter, things that are important, but do not deserve the amount of time you allocate for them. These include things like checking social media accounts at work or focusing on the agendas of other people instead of working on clearing your schedule for the day. By the end of the day, you will have wasted a lot of time and energy. Anything that has not been completed by close of business gets pushed to the next day, or the next week, and so forth.

You can also decide to take the perspective of competitor analysis. Study what your competition is doing. How are they going about their business? Study their strengths and weaknesses and understand how they are dealing with some of the challenges you are facing in the industry. From here, you can learn something meaningful that will help you rethink your priorities and achieve your long-term goals.

Identify Growth Drivers

Growth is an integral part of life. Whether you are looking at growth from a personal point of view or a corporate perspective, you need to grow from strength to strength. Everyone wants to improve. You want to wake up tomorrow in a better position financially than you were today. You want to be in a satisfying, better paying job three years down the line than where you are today. The same applies to companies. Companies want to expand their reach; they want to have more customers than those they have today.

Given this desire and obsession with growth, you need to discover the things that drive growth in the industry, and from a personal level, the things that inspire you to grow. Growth is about value addition. This is why you will realize that not all activities in the company are responsible for growth. There are some departments that the company can easily do away with when things are thick financially, and the company will still be okay.

Looking at things this way, what are you invested in for the company? Are you committed to performing duties in your department, functions that might not help the company make strides into the future? Look at the company objectives. Try to think about your current position in alignment with this. If you are sure you are not adding value to the company, you might want to think about pushing for a move into a department that makes those critical steps. You need to be part of something bigger, something that gives you purpose.

Doing the mundane things from time to time will only make you irrelevant. If you feel you are not making progress at a personal level, you should think about making wholesome changes. You need to rethink your strategies in life. Do away with anything that does not add value to your life. You might also need to consult an expert, a life coach or someone who has a better grip on their life than you do.

Making some of these changes might not be easy, neither will they be a one-person job. However, with the right guidance, you can get things done. Even as you try to set your priorities, do not overdo it.

Embrace Quality Communication

You need to communicate your priorities, especially if you are working within a team. This is important because it helps to resonate ideas. They stay fresh in the minds of your team. You avoid the scenario where people are working aimlessly, just for the sake of getting through the day. As we mentioned earlier, you need a purpose.

One of the reasons why most team leaders and their teams fail is because the leaders only communicate what is relevant in the boardroom. However, when they come to their teams, they barely communicate the priorities and goals. It is impossible for anyone to work well in the company when they barely understand what they are working towards. If your people are unable to link the work they are doing to the needs of the company, there exists a disconnect, and this will bring your team and the entire company down.

Assigning Timelines

While addressing priorities as urgent matters, not all of them are the same. Therefore, you should not allocate the same time to all of them. Some demand more effort and time than others. You should, however, make sure you have deadlines which you can meet.

Getting the right balance between what is more important than others is very difficult. Study all the items you have listed as priorities and understand what you need for each of them. From there, you can decide upon how to share your time across different tasks.

Appreciate Progress

It is important to realize how far you have come. However small the wins are, be sure to recognize and celebrate them. This gives you the morale to keep working to meet your goals. Whether you are working as a team, or putting in the effort as an individual, a pat on the back can give you the confidence you need to achieve more.

Even as you appreciate these wins, however, make sure you do not spend a lot of time wallowing in the moment. You have to move on so fast. You need to create momentum; you need to celebrate some of the strides you are making early enough in your route to success. You have to remember that each win is a sign that you are doing things right, and there is room for more.

You should not only look at this from the point of progress, but use it as an opportunity to look back and appreciate what you have achieved. Things will not always go according to plan. You have to prepare for that. Do not get so used to success that you struggle to cope at the first sight of failure or a stumbling block.

At this juncture, you also need enough time to reflect on yourself. Personally, what has this project you are undertaking done to you? Has it taken its toll on you? In that case, what can you do about it? If it is a project that you are undertaking with others, what is it doing to them?

What changes are happening in their lives? Is it changing their lives for the better, or are they having a difficult time adjusting?

If you are in charge of a team, it is essential to consider the welfare of your team members, because this eventually mirrors back to the project you are working on. If someone is having a difficult time, chances are high they will not deliver quality results on the project. The same sentiment applies to you too. Even at a personal level, if you are struggling with something in your life as a result of the project you are working on, you will struggle to give your best to the project. Therefore, to prioritize and meet your goals, you have to make sure you take care of yourself. You have to align personal well-being with the needs of the task at hand.

Priorities Can Change

At this juncture you have learned that priorities never stay the same. They change from time to time. Changing order of priorities is why you need to have a list of things to do. If you have a plan to meet specific goals by the end of the day, you cannot waste time on a task that you cannot complete for some reason. If it is beyond you, push it down the line and move on to the next thing on the list. Perhaps you need someone to be physically present to complete that task, yet they are away, and can only make it back to the office in the afternoon. It makes sense to put that task away until then.

Changing the order of priorities is not a bad thing either. You merely understand the fact that, by changing the order, you are focusing on the things that are more important, or achievable right away.

Stay True to Yourself

Even as you create a list of priorities, it is crucial that you do not run away from reality. How much time do you need to spend on tasks that you have set out to do? Do not try to make yourself invincible when you know it is not possible. Time is a limited resource. You might have other things to do during the day too.

It is easier to achieve your goals and set priorities if they are realistic. Assign the right time and deadlines to the tasks you need to accomplish. While it is essential to push yourself to work harder, smarter, and achieve so much more, you also have to be honest about what you can truly achieve. Do not confuse pushing yourself with putting unnecessary pressure on yourself.

Working with Mentors

There are so many things you might never know about yourself, your problems, or your situation, until you talk to someone. You have people in your life that you look up to. Consult these people from time to time. Discuss the progress you are making in life with them. They can help you get a different perspective and help you to see things more clearly. These are people who can challenge you to do more, to become a better version of yourself.

A mentor can help you in times when you are struggling to judge and determine the urgency of events, practicality, and feasibility. As you grow from strength to strength, it is possible to lose focus or direct your attention towards other things that probably do not matter. Losing sight of the ultimate goal is a reality you must face from time to time.

What a mentor does is help you to remember what you are working on. They help you remember your true purpose, what you set out to achieve from the onset. It is true that plans and priorities might have changed along the line, but one thing that never changes is your ultimate goal, your true purpose for whichever project you are undertaking. A mentor reminds you of the important things that matter. They make sure you do not lose yourself in the process.

Chapter 10: Sharpening Your Planning Goals

A lot of people leave goal setting and planning for the New Year. Soon after that, however, they fail to keep up with the goals they set in the first place. You must have come across this already. However, this is not about New Year resolutions; this is about getting you through your day, through your week and, more importantly, achieving all you have set out to do.

Without a plan in mind, it is virtually impossible to get anywhere. You would end up meandering aimlessly. Planning goes hand in hand with visions. What is your mission in life, in your workplace, for the day, and so forth? There are tiny little goals that you set for yourself which, when achieved, help you move closer and closer to your ultimate objectives.

You must have a plan already, to help you to achieve your goals. However, they do not seem to be working. What could you be missing? Where could you be going wrong? A good plan can fail if you do not enhance it. These ideas need to be reviewed and honed if they are to work for you.

Even in companies, you will evaluate and review plans from time to time. This is the only way they can be useful. Plans do not exist in isolation. For them to work, there are elements that must align in the environment within which you are implementing the plan. The same notion applies to your situation.

Do not come up with a plan and keep it static. Be ready to adjust it accordingly, where necessary. So, how do you sharpen your goals? What can you do to make them more efficient? Your goals have gotten you this far; now it is time to make sure they take you even further.

Brainstorm

Humans are social beings. We continuously thrive around others. It helps, therefore, that you brainstorm with like-minded fellows, in an attempt to learn more about how they handle things at their end. When it comes to brainstorming, it does not necessarily have to be with like-minded people. You learn new things each day, and you might learn a lesson or two from someone unexpected.

Talk to people in your immediate environment. You have probably seen how they go about their tasks. Ask them how they are where they are today. Find out about some of the challenges they encounter, and how they respond. Try not to be too intrusive, though. Most people do not like that, so watch out for the cues in your conversation with them.

The good thing about brainstorming is that you might have some challenges that are keeping you from meeting your goals, which you have never thought you could overcome. By talking to someone, you'd be surprised at how similar your situations are, and their perspective on that situation might help you to make the right changes in your life.

Focus on the Bigger Picture

Many are the times we set goals for ourselves and lose ourselves in the process of meeting the little milestones. These milestones are important, but never lose sight of the bigger picture. You will come across bumps along the road, but these should not prevent you from making progress.

You should keep a clear mind when going about this. Remind yourself from time to time what you are working towards, and why it is vital that you achieve it. The reminder will set you miles apart from everyone else, and as you scale the heights of success, use that to inspire others to become better too. In the end, you will be surrounding yourself with people who respect you, appreciate your contribution to their lives, and who will help you walk your path to success.

Take Notes

How often do you take notes? Note-taking is one of the simplest ways of improving your planning goals, but very few people seem to take it seriously. From the moment you were a child in the early learning stages, teachers reminded you of the importance of taking notes. It does not end with your final exams. Taking notes is an essential part of life and will help you to become a better person.

Note-taking gives you something to refer to. You can reflect upon the notes at the end of the day, find where you went wrong, what you can do about it, and so forth. The good thing about technology today is that there are so many ways of taking notes. If you do it digitally, keep the notes synchronized in your devices so that you can refer to them later on.

Part of taking notes is to help you stay focused. Taking notes enables you to make sure that influences from outside influence none of your goals. You set the goals and keep working towards meeting them.

Organization

For you to sharpen your goals, you have to be organized. Organization means you realize you have a mammoth task ahead of you, and you find a way of achieving it. Success is no sprint; it is a marathon. You have to go the extra mile to beat the rest. More importantly, you have to work harder to conquer the personal adversity inside you.

More often it is your inhibitions that hold you back from realizing your real potential. Break down your goals into manageable milestones. Set a plan in motion so that one thing leads to another. This way, each accomplished goal will get you closer to your ultimate goal.

With micro-goals, it is easier to realize the challenges or tasks in your life that you cannot accomplish on your own. This will also enable you to realize when, where, and how you need help, and how to get it. It is okay to ask for help. There is no shame in it – the moment you recognize and appreciate this, you will be open to healthy collaboration with people who can help you realize your real potential.

Vision Boards

Why do people create vision boards? You have probably come across this so many times. You have been advised often to consider creating a vision board of your own. You can create a physical vision board, a digital one, or as some people do, have one in your mind. Whichever works for you is best.

Vision boards will act as an inspiration for you whenever you meet goals, overcome challenges, and achieve some of the items on your vision board. It is a constant reminder that nothing is too difficult to achieve. It will also remind you of some of the obstacles that you had to overcome to get to where you are, and this would be an excellent motivator.

Invest in Yourself

In your quest to become a better person, a successful

individual, you try so many things you eventually forget to invest in the one thing that truly matters – yourself. You have to take good care of yourself, mentally, physically, and otherwise. Without this, all your efforts will go to waste. What use is your success if you cannot be there to revel in it?

How often do you exercise? Do you drink a lot of water? How would you define the relationships you have with people around you? Do you spare time to think and have some clarity by yourself? For someone who lives by the beach, do you ever find time to take a brisk walk along the beach in the evening or early in the morning? Are you eating right?

These are some simple things that you might be taking for granted, but in the long run, they will mean a lot. You have to stay refreshed, energized, and focused on tackling each day. This will make the difference between yourself and others around you. Get sufficient sleep. Invest in a good set of pillows, linen, and so forth. Make sure you are getting not just sufficient sleep, but quality sleep.

Maintain a routine. I cannot stress this more than enough times. Keep a routine and stick to it. Routines help you create good habits that eventually become a part of who you are. Spare time for family and friends. This is the time that you set aside to interact with them, to talk to them, and share in their experiences. Keep your devices away from you during this time. Nurture your body, and you will be strong and healthy enough to enjoy the fruits of your success.

How to Achieve Your Goals

When you are just starting, things might look fuzzy. It feels like you are working on a gigantic puzzle. You know what the result is supposed to look like, but you do not know how to get there. You have thousands of pieces to put together, and it feels like a mammoth task. You have an idea of the end goal. What you need is a plan for how to get there.

Find Your Purpose

For you to work on something and deliver the best results, you need to work on something you love. If you do not enjoy it, you will never be passionate about it. So, the question you should be asking yourself is, what matters to you? What do you want out of this?

There is a lesson in human resource management that monetary gains are not motivating factors. It is true. Money comes and goes. However, the personal attachment you have to your goals, your reason for waking up and putting in hours and hours of effort, is a different story altogether. Money is just one of the rewards you get for doing what you do.

To sharpen your goals and move closer to realizing your dream, you should never lose focus of what matters to you. This might be the reason why you started working on what you are. Never lose sight of this. If possible, write it down somewhere. Put it on a frame and pin it on the wall in your office. Your vision should be a constant reminder of why you started this. It should also remind you of how far you have come, and how much more you need to do.

SWOT Analysis

The mention of a SWOT analysis usually elicits thoughts of a comparative study between companies. However, when planning your goals, this is just as important. When you study companies to determine their strengths, weaknesses, opportunities, and existing threats in the environments within which they operate, what you are mostly trying to do is understand that company better.

You are trying to know what works for them, why they do what they do, and whether it makes sense for them to keep doing so. You are looking for opportunities that they can take advantage of, and become the next big thing in the industry. You are looking at the stimuli in their environment that threaten their very existence, which they should be wary of. You are studying the business environment within which the company operates, and by the end of it, you have a rough projection of the best course of action for the company. You should use this concept when planning your goals.

Take yourself as a case study like a company. You must conduct a SWOT analysis to understand yourself better. Be very honest while you are at it. You know your strengths and weaknesses. You can even consult people around you to confirm some of these features. Next, you need to think about your environment. What are the opportunities that you feel you can take advantage of in your immediate environment? What will happen if you take your chances when afforded the opportunity?

Before jumping to conclusions and investing in something, address the threats too. For an entrepreneur, success is the goal, but there is also the risk of failure. What happens if you fail? Do you have a fallback plan? Do you have cushions in place if, for example, a global financial meltdown occurs again? Do you feel you can handle the pressure that comes with failure?

You must be very honest in these assessments because they will help you to make plans to achieve your goals, and map your vision for the future.

Daily Planning

Even with an efficient plan worked out, you still need to make sure you plan each day. Looking at the bigger picture, you already have a plan in place. What you need are smaller plans that will help you tackle each day. Most successful people work with routines, which are simple plans they carry out every morning.

From the time they wake up, things are set in motion. They have a morning schedule, things they must do before leaving the house, things they do immediately after they get to their offices, and things they do in the evening before sleeping.

Daily planning is an integral part of helping you achieve the greater goal. Try to plan and schedule your days accordingly. Spare a few minutes every morning for this or set aside time in the evening before you go to sleep.

Plan your day on paper. You might have an idea of what you need to do tomorrow but penning it on paper makes it more realistic. This should remind you of what you need to do.

Chapter 11: Planning Ahead and Avoiding Distractions

Distractions are common in the workplace, and for different reasons. When you fail to plan, you will struggle to stay focused throughout the day. Your success is determined by how well you can plan and manage your time.

Time management is about organizing your time between some of the challenging tasks you have to accomplish by the end of the day. A critical aspect of time management is planning. If you have a plan and you stick to it, there is very little you will struggle to do. Hard work is overrated. To succeed in life, you have to be smart about the way you work.

Hard workers spend a lot of time sweating and toiling, to make sure people see them putting in the hours. Smart workers, on the other hand, do so much in very little time. Even when you are running out of time and the pressure to deliver is intense, your effectiveness depends on how well you manage your time.

Spare the time to talk to some of the high achievers you know. One thing common between all of them is how well they manage their time. You have to be exceptionally good at this. You should be a result-oriented person.

There are benefits of proper planning that you can look forward to, including reduced stress, being able to use the opportunities that come your way, an improved professional outlook, efficiency, productivity, and confidence.

If you cannot manage your time well, some challenges will become part and parcel of your day. These include things like poor quality of work, missing deadlines, inefficiency, increased stress, a stalled career, and a deteriorating professional reputation. Very soon, no one will want to associate with you.

The lessons you learn in time management and planning are things that will help you for the rest of your life. The experiences are not just about your career, but also about your personal life. These are lessons you can also share with your loved ones, your children, and coworkers.

How can you manage your time properly such that distractions become a thing of the past? How do you become impenetrable to distractions, internal, personal, electronic or otherwise? Here are some useful ideas that will help you to establish boundaries during work hours, and eliminate the risk of procrastination.

Personal Accountability

While a lot of distractions are external, most disturbances are internal. These are the ones that weigh you down the most. Are you okay? Have you ever taken time to figure things out?

Life is hard as it is, and you might be going through a lot with no one to talk to about things. You are probably feeling flighty and anxious. If something is bothering you and taking away your peace and tranquility, get to the bottom of it. The emotional trauma can manifest and grow into something worse, making it difficult for you to focus on anything else.

Identify the Sources of Distraction

If you are in a good place, you have no personal concerns drawing your attention from work or your schedules, then you might have an external distraction problem. Dealing with external distraction is easy. You merely need to identify them and shut them out.

Perhaps it is one of your co-workers getting in your

space. Maybe the office setup is in such a way that you cannot maintain your focus. If there is something you can do about it, changes that you can make, go ahead and make them. These changes can help you get rid of distractions.

Preparation

Take your time and read about some of the great leaders in the world. You will notice they always have planners working on their payroll. A professional planner might not be affordable for you, but you can still get your preparations in order.

With this in mind, you can complete all your tasks on time. You have a list of things that you need to do. Write these down, and plan for all of them. Highlight the necessary steps and procedure for handling such tasks. Preparing ahead of your day should save you a lot of time.

Clear Your Workstation

Disorganization is not just a state of your mind; it can also come as a result of the physical state of your workplace. Most people have a very disorganized workstation. You have files all over the place, all sorts of items call your desk home. There might even be so many things on your desk that you cannot remember to whom they belong, but for some reason, you are comfortable seeing them on your desk.

Someone who has a disorganized desk will almost always be disorganized at work. Your desk will be a source of distraction, not just for yourself, but also for your workmates. People will never run out of things to say about your desk. If someone passes by, they will want to touch something or tell you something about it.

Creating such a convenient stop-over for your fellow employees is an easy way to become distracted and not get anything done. It starts with one person stopping by to make a light conversation with you, and the next thing you know, your desk is the convening point for all random office gossip. People go for their tea breaks, grab a cup of coffee and pass by your desk for a brief conversation. Get your desk organized and you will have made the right step towards fighting distractions at work.

Keep Your Door Shut

If you are lucky to work in an office plan that is not open, make use of your door. Close the door if you are not attending to someone. Go about your work in silence. Most offices these days favor open office plans. Shutting the door behind you allows you the freedom to work in peace, away from distractions by your workmates.

You will realize you are spending less time distracted than when you leave your door open. Besides, when the door is open, it is always an open invitation for anyone who wishes to run something by you to come in and have a chat with you. You will end up dealing with a lot of random walk-in meetings, at the expense of your productivity.

Working Offline

Even though a lot of people claim they have to be online at work, this is not always necessary. You will probably only need to be online when checking and sending emails, or researching something. Unless you need to be online, you have no business being online.

Going offline does not just work for your office laptop, but it also applies to your phone and any other gadget you are using. Stay off the internet until you have finished the task you set out to accomplish, then you can go online and catch up on all the random items that interest you.

Taking Breaks

Do you have plans to take a break away from work? Have you ever done this? Most people cannot remember. Immediately you get to work in the morning, you barely get a breather.

The strain can get to you and put you under pressure. You should know when to take a break. Relax a bit if things are not working. Take a walk. Reassess your position, unwind, and come back when you see things more clearly.

Listening to Music

Ever heard some people say music makes everything better? It is true. At times all you need is to plug your earphones in, play some music and get lost in your work.

Playing music has proven to be useful for a lot of people. These days it is not uncommon to walk into an office setting and find people with earphones plugged into their ears.

If you have noise canceling headphones, this will be much better. Music tends to give you peace. Choose the type of music you use during work carefully, though. Some music might make you drift further away from the task you are performing, and even distract you more than the distractions you are trying to avoid.

There are different types of music that you can use to help you focus when you are at work. You can listen to white noise, for example. Some people work well with the sound of rain playing in the background, an endless loop or birds chirping in the morning, waves at sea, and so forth. The good thing about this is that all this is available on YouTube. You can also download and create a playlist on your device if you are worried about your discipline when you sign into YouTube.

Improve Your Concentration

It is not easy to concentrate on a task for a very long

time, especially if it is a huge one. You should learn a thing or two about how to manage this. One of the most straightforward options is to break the task into smaller units.

With a smaller task, you need a very short attention span to get it done. Do this for all the mini-tasks you have created, and you will find yourself focusing on and completing the task faster, and with fewer distractions.

Set and Implement Deadlines

Setting deadlines for the work you are doing is another way of dealing with distractions. With deadlines to beat, you have to work hard to make sure you accomplish the task on time. You cannot afford to waste time. You know that if you do not make it on time, there will be repercussions.

Deadlines give you an end to look forward to. It gets even better if there is a reward at the end. The brain naturally appreciates rewards. Therefore, it is easier to push everything aside and channel all your effort towards meeting deadlines.

Working After Hours

A lot of workplaces today are allowing their employees the freedom to choose their working hours. You can consider this in case your regular work hours are too demanding, or you find yourself struggling to make things work.

Nobody knows your work better than you do. You know the fellows who always make it difficult for anyone to focus. You know the people you cannot have around you when you are working on something serious.

You can beat the system by scheduling your work hours for a time when you cannot interact with these people. For the challenging tasks, try coming in during the weekends to get them done. It is often quieter and more peaceful during this time since a lot of people are busy relaxing at home or engaged in social activities. Another option is to come in early or sacrifice some hours in the evening to get things done.

Coming in earlier is a better option, though. You are fresh and full of energy in the morning. If you can maintain the focus when you come in at least one hour ahead of time, you can keep this up for most of the tasks you need to accomplish during the day. Try to keep the positive energy and vibes flowing. Do not let it dissipate before you utilize it fully.

Chapter 12: Procrastination

At some point in time, you have been a victim of procrastination. Procrastination is a challenge the entire human race has had to deal with for a very long time. Putting things off because you do not want to deal with them yet, or you are not ready to face them. People always have a credible reason for procrastination. This is one of those moments of denial where you know you haven't done the right thing, but you have a ready excuse. Procrastination is to act against your better judgment. You find yourself doing something when you know you should be doing some other thing altogether. It is also losing self-control.

Why Do You Procrastinate?

Procrastination is all about what goes on in your brain. Behavioral scientists have studied procrastination for a long time and have determined that, despite your intentions to do something else, procrastination seems to pull you in against your better judgment. There is a time inconsistency that manifests in the brain. With this time inconsistency, your brain appreciates immediate rewards far more than future rewards.

Procrastination is a constant war within yourself, about acting and meeting your future goals. When making plans for the future, you feel good about them. You look forward to achieving those goals. However, instead of addressing those plans, you think you are better off doing something else.

It is about instant gratification. You want something good, and you want it right now. It feels much better than having to wait for it. Take the example of working out. You have made plans to lose weight and get into the frame you have always wanted. However, to do this, you have to stay away from certain types of food, which you love so much. Each time you come across these foods, you cannot help but stop to take a bite, and assure yourself that you will start the workout regimen the next day. This is the last time you are eating unhealthy food. You make this promise to yourself over and over again until you give up altogether, and resign yourself to not making it at all.

The same applies when you are in your younger, more productive years. You know putting money aside will help you save for the future. However, the future is more than 50 years away. It feels so much better spending money on a concert or buying a PlayStation, so you get immediate satisfaction. Your brain appreciates instant gratification more than expected future returns.

Overcoming Procrastination

Everyone has put something off at a given time in their life. Some people might call you lazy, but that is not it. What you are tackling is bigger than laziness. You should understand it, and try to find ways of dealing with it. You find yourself thinking you have a lot of time to do something when in the real sense you do not.

Psychologists believe there is an element of task aversion linked to procrastination. When you feel a particular task will be too difficult to handle, it is easier for you to set it aside, instead of going on with it. You might be trying to escape the distress associated with handling that task, but in the long run, you only succeed at causing more problems. If the task was yours to perform, you would still have to face it head-on. You might even have to deal with it under a lot of unnecessary pressure.

The problem with procrastination is that, after a while, it becomes a habitual vice. You might be so badly off you cannot do anything else. If something does not satisfy them instantly, they put it off. You do not want to be that person. There are health concerns associated with procrastination that you do not want to happen to you. Stress and poor performance are just the obvious ones.

Your confidence also takes a hit because no one trusts you to get anything done anymore. Your self-worth goes down the drain. It gets to a point where you do not trust yourself to get things done. You will end up wallowing in self-pity, struggling with shame and guilt.

Dealing with Procrastination

If you notice you have been having a difficult time getting things done, you need to make structural changes to get things done. It might be an uphill task, but making a start will get you going. Here are some tips to assist.

Stop Making Excuses

If excuses are a regular part of your life, stop making them. Learn to own up to your mistakes. Take responsibility for your actions. You do not have to wait for something to happen before you start doing what you should. Take the initiative and get going.

Try to be honest. Most of the time you think you are lying to others, yet in the real sense, you are only lying to yourself, to make you feel good about something that is not even real. Do not wait to get in the mood. Do not wait to get in the zone. All you are doing is delaying your work or project further.

Partner Up!

In your endeavor to stop procrastination, getting a partner for a given task might help you a lot. Having a partner enables you to be efficient. A partner holds you accountable for your actions. They call you out when you are lazy.

The secret is to choose a partner that can keep you on your toes. You can pick someone you look up to, someone you never want to disappoint, or someone you hold in high regard. It could be your immediate supervisor, a coach, or even your co-workers.

Set deadlines for the work you need to get done and work towards getting that done. You must also create accountability times when you provide reports on progress.

These are times when you get in touch with your partner to update them on the progress you have made. Since you do not want to go back on your word or disappoint them, this will help you to push yourself to get things done.

Remember that choosing the right partner will help you to succeed. Do not select someone you can bully or someone you can easily talk into leniency. Your partner needs to be a steadfast person, one who has perspective.

Stop Catastrophizing

You find yourself making a big deal out of everything, and this should stop. You always think about how painful it might be for you to complete a given task, or how difficult it will be, how boring it is, and so forth. The more you do this, the more unbearable you will find the task.

None of these things you worry about will kill you. So what if the task is tedious? So what if you feel tired at the end of it? You are still alive. You will not even fall sick. Delaying these tasks, however, might make you sick. Procrastination could lead to stress when you have so much to do and very little time to work with. What you need to do might not be one of your favorite tasks, but you have to do it.

Division of Labor

If you have a task to complete and it is too big, there is a good chance you will always push it aside. You do this hoping to find enough time to do it, but you rarely do. Before you know it, the deadline is fast approaching, and you cannot even find a way to start working on it.

Any manager would tell you the best way to get some of these things done is to divide and conquer. Split the task into phases and complete them one at a time. As you do this, remember how far you have come, and you will appreciate your effort and keep working harder to complete the task altogether.

Where possible, share the task with people around you. Some functions call for a collaborative effort if you are to succeed in accomplishing them. Since different people are working on it, the need to push the task to a later date does not arise. Besides, you will not feel overwhelmed by the job. Instead, you will be looking forward to getting it done.

Get a Different Perspective

A common theme in procrastination is the desire for short-term benefits over long-term results. Take a different perspective. Ask yourself, why are you getting this done? What is in it for you?

Imagine, for a moment, completing the task you have been putting off for a while. Imagine that invoice clearing – the money would feel so good resting in your account, right? Picture yourself buying that new bike you have been saving up for.

If you start thinking about the result, it is easier to work even harder to get things done. You might also put in more hours to accomplish tasks faster, and better. Taking on a different perspective is essential as it helps you have positive vibes oozing around you. You are more confident this way, and you become a better role model for people you associate with.

Be Real

Build a routine, create a schedule and follow it, to help you deal with procrastination. This is a good thing, only if you do it right. Some people get things wrong from the very beginning. As you craft your schedule, try to make sure it is properly aligned.

Do not create a schedule that ends up looking like you are superhuman. Be realistic about your breaks. Be honest with yourself about the things you can fit into that schedule. Do not put too much on your plate so that you look like you are the busiest person on the planet.

You also have to be honest about your energy levels. You know you are not a morning person – why on earth are you scheduling demanding tasks for the morning? This is to help you get results, not to impress people. You cannot achieve your goals if you are not honest with yourself.

Protect Your Environment

Some elements around you encourage procrastination. Disruptive technology is all around you, and some of the tech you access only succeed at disrupting your focus. Just because someone has reached out to you on email does not mean you have to respond to them right away. Just because you have a WhatsApp group with your workmates where you talk about your horrible bosses does not mean you have to be on the group chatting at the earliest convenience – even if you are the group administrator.

These are some of the things that lead you astray. You soon run out of time, the day is gone, and you have not achieved anything. Your boss will always be horrible, and they will be even meaner when you are not meeting your deliverables.

Most devices today come with a Do Not Disturb feature. You can customize this to suit your work interests. Create new profiles for different scenarios, so that at the push of a button, you turn off everything that might distract you when you are busy. Better yet, keep your devices out of sight.

Chapter 13: Making the Most of Your Time

The world we live in is moving at a breakneck pace. It is easy to get carried away and lose yourself in the process, and you find yourself unable to meet your goals. No generation before us has enjoyed a better use of technology than we have. Technology influences lifestyle changes in an innovative way that it is virtually impossible not being able to interact with tech, or experience the disruptions.

One thing that is obvious at the moment is the importance of time. Compared to our parents and other generations before us, we are struggling to accomplish a lot of things. This leaves you wondering how to make the most use of the little time you have on your hands.

Before looking into ways of being very productive and making the most use of your time, here are some realities that you must appreciate about your time:

- Things have changed. You end up struggling to accomplish a lot much earlier in life than you would have had to a few years ago.

- Time is a limited resource. Yes, you read that right. Time is running out, and you have to try to utilize it wisely.

- The value of time. You cannot place value on the time you have. You, therefore, should learn how to control it, use it well and unleash your potential.

- Time is an asset. As an asset, time is a tool at your disposal. You can save it, share it, divide it, manipulate it in any way you want.

Productivity is the ultimate goal most people struggle with every single day. You have things to do, you have targets to beat, aims to achieve, and so forth. You have a lot of things to do, but very little time. How can you go about this? How do you make sure you can achieve all you need to without feeling the strain?

Some methods have always worked for successful people in the past. Your case is no different. What might not be the same is their implementation methods. Case scenarios might not be the same, but the ultimate goal, managing your time, might be the same. Find useful ideas herein that can make you go the extra mile, making the most use of your time:

Planning

Planning is probably one of the first things anyone will tell you about time. You have to plan for it. Like any other resource, you must prepare adequately for your time. If you cannot, you will end up unable to account for how you spend yours.

You can make plans either before you sleep or early in the morning when you wake up. You can organize your day properly and make plans for an entire week ahead of time. Planning seldom takes more than 30 minutes.

In this plan, you should have the day organized from the moment you wake up to the time you go to bed. Do not be rigid in your program, and at the same time, do not be too flexible. If you make your plans too strict, the slightest change might set you off track. If you keep your plans too flexible, it becomes easy for you to veer off course, since you have a lot of room to maneuver.

Planning calls for discipline, as does execution. If you are disciplined, you will do a lot of things in good time, and will not have time to waste. One of the benefits of making the most use of your time is that, if done correctly, you end up with a lot of time on your hands at the end of the day.

You have enough time left over for you to rest, spend time with the family, read a book, or do anything that makes you a better person.

Managing Yourself

If you cannot manage time correctly, you might fail to manage the one thing that matters perhaps more than time: yourself. You need breaks in between your packed schedule. You need time to relax, time to catch a breather. When planning your program for the day, be very keen on the tasks that demand a lot of energy. Packing these closely together will be detrimental to you in the long run.

You should space out your plan, so you do not wear yourself out. Set timelines for your schedules. Try to spend only the necessary time on your assignments. If you feel it will take too much time and eat into the time set aside for something else, reconsider and move onto the next item on your list. This way, you do not end up with backlogs or wasting time on something that is unachievable.

The most important thing about planning for your time is making sure that, in between your schedules, you find time to take care of yourself. Have time for a meal, spare time to stretch your legs a bit, or get some fresh air.

Setting Priorities

There is a reason why you have an order of performing some tasks ahead of others. These are priority tasks. Address priorities ahead of everything else. You might not like them, but they are crucial. Accomplishing them as early as possible, and when you have adequate time to rest will go a long way.

It is always advisable that you handle your priority tasks when you are alert mentally and when you are calm. This way, you can deal with them well and give them all the attention they deserve.

Completing such tasks on the right footing further gives you a spring in your step. You are more confident when you have handled challenging tasks competently, and you can carry this into the rest of your day. Nothing can hold you back.

Stay Focused

Losing focus of your goals for the day is easy. There are so many distractions around you, and succumbing to them will give you problems. You do not always have to respond to everything that happens around you. You have to remind yourself that you are working on something that is more important than anything else.

Trust Your Instinct

One of the other reasons why you end up struggling to account for your time is second-guessing your moves. You should learn how to do things once. Do not get in the habit of delaying decision making, or taking a long time thinking about what to do.

Indecision is a big problem for a lot of people, especially when dealing with tasks that do not necessarily seem to be priority tasks. Try to complete everything you are working on before you start doing something new.

The Importance of Delegation

You might not have the capacity to do everything on your own even if you try to convince yourself that you are invincible. It is impossible for you to handle everything on your own. At some point, you have to relax a little and share some of the work with those around you.

There is nothing wrong with sharing some of your work. It is not a sign of weakness, but a means of making sure nothing is left undone. Besides, you cannot be perfect at everything. By delegating some of your work to people who are more capable, you are ensuring all work receives the attention it deserves.

This is the principle of specialization, which all entrepreneurs understand too well. It is better to share the task with someone who is an expert at it than leaving it to someone who tries their hand at everything. Sharing some work with people who are good at what they do is not just about completing the task, but it is also about getting a different perspective.

The work environment is supposed to be about collaboration. You share ideas with people, and in the process, you can learn so much. If you are in charge of the workforce, you should know your workers well enough to understand what their strengths and weaknesses are, respective of your goals and objectives for each task. If you belong to any team, you should do the same with your teammates. Understanding what they are good at will go a long way towards helping you succeed together as a team, saving you a lot of time in the process.

Slow Down

It is easy to get caught up in a rush to meet and beat your deadlines and targets, to the point where you lose yourself in the process. As you get through the day, it is essential that you learn how and when to slow down and get a breather. Slowing down is a good way for you to get a better perspective of what you are doing.

Slowing down should give you a better insight or perspective into the day and what you are working for. It is like taking a trip through a forest. If you drive by, you will be in and out of the woods in a few minutes, and you will barely appreciate the sight. However, if you walk through the forest, you will have the best view, and you will also feel rejuvenated, happier, and enjoy the fresh air. Slowing down will help you take a step back and understand why you are doing things. It gives you purpose. It helps you to stay focused and remember the reason why you are doing what you are.

Account for Your Time

Taking stock of your time at the end of the day helps you understand where your time went. This way, you know how you spent the day, which tasks were challenging, and helps you plan for others that are repetitive, but challenging.

To account for your time, consider keeping a diary. A diary becomes useful because you know exactly how and where you spent your time all through the day. Writing this down also helps you realize time gaps in your day, things or areas where you waste a lot of time, and come up with ideas for improving that.

Noting things down will also help you identify trends and patterns and how they manifest. You will determine the times of the day when you are most productive, and when your burnout starts to show. It will also help you understand whether you are meeting your priorities as you set them out each day.

It is like watching a game on TV, and then at the end of the game, pundits give an analysis of the game. They discuss the game from the beginning to the end. They look at some of the controversial decisions in the game. They highlight the errors that players made, some of the magical moments in the game. More importantly, they emphasize progress since the previous game, and any changes that were made by the coaches to their teams, and the results of that.

This is the same thing you will be doing. You analyze your day. There is no one better placed to do this than yourself. After all, you understand your day better because you lived it. You look back at your decisions, you look at the progress you have made the entire week, and decide how you want to proceed in the coming days.

Conclusion

Managing time is an essential aspect of success that you cannot take for granted. If you have goals and aspirations in life, you need to start working on them right away. Plan your days accordingly.

You now know some of the things that distract you each day, things that contribute to the time you lose. This is time you will never get back. What you can do is plan for the time you have right now, and the time ahead of you. Do away with distractions. Do not just declutter your desk, declutter your schedule and life.

Identify the relationships to which you belong. Define them and end those that do not add value to your life. These are some of the things that are holding you back and keeping you from reaching your potential. You might not like the fallback, but in a few days or weeks, you will notice the difference, and you will appreciate the decision to walk away.

Only one person is holding you back, and you look at that person each day when you stand in front of your mirror. Challenge yourself to do things differently, to do things better than you have done before. It is possible. It has been done before. People are doing it all the time. Why not you? The path to success might not be an easy one to walk, but you can streamline it and make it manageable. The sacrifices you make right now will eventually pay off.

Your time is invaluable, and you can utilize it properly. The tips you have learned in this book will go a long way and make you an efficient member of whichever team you work with. You will have a defined purpose in life and know how to work on your goals.

Good Luck!

www.ingramcontent.com/pod-product-compliance
Lightning Source LLC
Chambersburg PA
CBHW071641080526
44586CB00013BA/1198
* 9 7 8 1 9 8 9 1 2 0 1 3 2 *